Enjoy!

The World's Funniest Internet Jokes

VOLUME I

Col. Charles H. Booth, Jr.

I-FORM INK PUBLISHING

Published by
I-Form Ink Publishing
40960 Avenida Rosario
Palm Desert, California 92260

Library of Congress Control Number: 2014919278
ISBN: 978-0-9763274-8-6

Printed in the United States of America by Morris Publishing®
3212 East Highway 30
Kearney, NE 68847
1-800-650-7888

ACKNOWLEDGEMENTS

I want to give credit to all my friends and acquaintances who over the years have shared some of these stories and jokes with me.

Among these are John Johnson, Ed Batz, Irene Parks, John Walker, Bob Walker, Russell Evans, Col. Larry Toney, Dick Hansen, Dan Snyder, Beebe Nauert, Carol Hensley, Ron Klink, John Framel, Gary Schultz, Lynn Ramage, Don Kobally, John & Maxine Dykstra, Donna Speer, Jean Weil, Ian Healy, John Hacker, Reid Rotzler, Karen Simmerman, Moira Davison, Karl Vacek, Red Stein, J.P. Monteverde, Ed Gottshalk, Bob Salathe, Eileen Kopelman, Tad Potter, Jenifer Salatka, Doc Ramage, Bob Capretta, Rose Monteleone, Tom Sifferman, Charley Friday, Bill Harbaugh, Bob Weil, Jim Ryan, Shari Erickson, Leslie Santucci, Jim Isbell, Jr., and many other good friends.

When they read the material and recognize it, I hope they laugh and take pleasure that it is being shared with others.

I also want to thank my dear wife, Trudi, for all of her encouragement to publish this book.

In addition, a special thanks to Julie Gorges, who edited this book, and to "Bud" Charles Gibbons for the cover artwork.

CONTENTS

CHAPTER

ONE

DRINK UP!

These jokes are offered up in the same spirit as Dean Martin, who often used drinking as a stage prop. Impersonating a debonair boozer with a nonchalant attitude, no one was more laid back or surpassingly cool than Martin.

By the way, although drinking was a running joke with the Rat Pack, his son, Ricci, wrote in a memoir that what looked like scotch in Martin's drinks onstage was usually apple juice.

So get ready, here we go!

A Jar of Olives

McQuillan walked into a bar and ordered martini after martini, each time removing the olives and placing them in a jar. When the jar was filled with olives and all the drinks consumed, the Irishman started to leave.

"S'cuse me", said a customer, who was puzzled over what McQuillan had done. "What was that all about?"

"Nothing," said the Irishman. "My wife just sent me out for a jar of olives."

Irish Prayer

Murphy was staggering home with a pint of booze in his back pocket when he slipped and fell heavily. Struggling to his feet, he felt something wet running down his leg.

"Please Lord," he implored, "let it be blood!"

You've Been Out Drinking Again

An Irishman had been drinking at a pub all night. The bartender finally said that the bar was closing. The Irishman stood up to leave and fell flat on his face. He tried to stand one more time with the same result. He figured he'd crawl outside and get some fresh air and maybe that would sober him up.

Once outside, he stood up and fell on his face again. So he decided to crawl the four blocks home. When he arrived at the door he stood up and fell flat on his face. He crawled through the door and into his bedroom.

When he reached his bed he tried one more time to stand up. This time he managed to pull himself upright, but he quickly fell right into the bed and was sound asleep as soon as his head hit the pillow.

He was awakened the next morning to his wife standing over him, shouting, "SO YOU'VE BEEN DRINKING AGAIN!"

Putting on an innocent look, intent on bluffing it out, he asked, "What makes you say that?"

"The pub just called; you left your wheelchair there again."

An Irishman Named O'Malley

An Irishman named O'Malley went to his doctor after a long illness.

The doctor sighed and looked O'Malley in the eye and said, "I've some bad news for you. You have cancer, and it can't be cured. You'd best put your affairs in order."

O'Malley was shocked but, being a solid character, he managed to compose himself and walk from the doctor's office into the waiting room where his son was waiting.

"Well son, we Irish celebrate when things are good and we celebrate when things don't go well. In this case, things aren't so well. I have cancer. Let's head to the pub and have a few pints."

After three or four pints, the two were feeling a little less somber. There were some laughs and some more beers. They were eventually approached by some of O'Malley's friends, who were curious as to what the two were celebrating. O'Malley told them they were drinking to his impending end.

"I have been diagnosed with AIDS," he told his friends.

The friends gave O'Malley their condolences, and they had a couple of more beers.

After the friends left, O'Malley's son leaned over and whispered in confusion, "Dad, I thought you told me that you were dying of cancer, and you just told you friends that you were dying of AIDS!"

O'Malley said, "I don't want any of them sleeping with your mother after I am gone."

It Pays to Turn on the Lights!

A good ol' boy, staggered home late on New Year's Eve after another evening with his drinking buddies. With his shoes in his left hand to avoid waking his wife, he tiptoed as quietly as he could toward the stairs leading to their upstairs bedroom.

However, he misjudged the bottom step in the darkened entryway. As he caught himself by grabbing the bannister, his body swung around and he landed heavily on his rump. A whiskey bottle in each back pocket broke and made the landing especially painful.

Managing to surpass a yelp, he sprung up, pulled down his pants, and examined his lacerated and bleeding cheeks in the mirror of a nearby darkened hallway. He managed to find a large box of band aids and proceeded to patch the wounds as best he could on any place he saw blood.

After hiding the now almost empty box, he managed to shuffle and stumble his way to bed. In the morning, he awakened with screaming pain in his head and his butt. He found his wife staring at him from across the room.

"You were drunk again last night," she stated.

Forcing himself to ignore his agony, he looked meekly at her and replied, "Now, honey, why would you say such a mean thing?"

"Well," she said, "there is the front door left open, the glass at the bottom of the stairs, and drops of blood trailing through the house, and your bloodshot eyes, but mostly it's all those band aids stuck on the downstairs mirror!"

Alcohol Warnings

Due to the increasing products liability litigation, American liquor manufacturers have accepted the FDA's suggestion that the following warning labels be placed immediately on all varieties of alcohol containers:

WARNING: Consumption of alcohol may lead you to believe that ex-lovers are really dying for you to telephone them at four in the morning.

WARNING: Consumption of alcohol is a major factor in dancing like an idiot.

WARNING: Consumption of alcohol may make you think you're whispering when you are not.

WARNING: Consumption of alcohol may lead you to think people are laughing WITH you.

WARNING: Consumption of alcohol may cause you to wake up with breath that could knock a buzzard off a dead animal one hundred yards away.

WARNING: Consumption of alcohol may cause an influx in the time-space continuum, whereby small (and sometimes large) gaps of time may seem to disappear.

WARNING: Consumption of alcohol may cause you to thay shings like thish.

WARNING: Consumption of alcohol may cause you to tell the same boring story over and over again until your friends want to assault you.

WARNING: Consumption of alcohol may cause you to think you can hold a logical conversation with members of the opposite sex without spitting.

WARNING: Consumption of alcohol may cause you to roll over in the morning and see something really scary.

WARNING: Consumption of alcohol may create the illusion that you are tougher, handsomer, and smarter than some really, really big guy named Psycho Bob.

Sue Happy

Somewhere in the Deep South, Bubba called an attorney and asked, "Is it true folks are suing cigarette companies for causing people to get cancer?"

"Yes, Bubba that's true," the lawyer answered.

"And people are suing the fast food restaurants for making them fat and clogging their arteries with all them burgers and fries," Bubba said. "Is that true?"

"Sure is, Bubba, but why do you ask?"

"Cause I was thinking maybe I can sue Budweiser for all them ugly women I been waken' up with."

Grandma's Fine!

Three guys were sitting in a biker bar. A man came in, already drunk, sat down at the bar, and ordered a drink.

The man looked around and saw the three men sitting at a corner table. He got up, staggered to the table, leaned over, looked the biggest one in the face and said, "I went by your grandma's house and I saw her in the hallway, buck naked. Man, she is fine!"

The biker looked at him and didn't say a word. His buddies were confused, because he was a bad ass, and would fight at the drop of a hat.

The drunk leaned on the table again and said, "I got it on with your grandma and she is good, the best I ever had!" The biker still said nothing.

His buddies were starting to get mad. The drunk leaned on the table again and said, "I'll tell you something else boy, your grandma liked it!"

The biker stood up, took the drunk by the shoulder and said, "Damn it, Grandpa, you're drunk! Go home!"

Three Times Is Not the Charm

An obnoxious drunk stumbles into the front door of a bar and orders a drink. The bartender says, "No way, buddy, you're too drunk."

A few minutes later, the drunk comes in though the bathroom. Again he slurs, "Give me a drink," and the bartender says, "No, man, I told you last time, you're too drunk."

Five minutes later, the guy comes in though the back door and orders a drink. Again the bartender says, "You're too drunk."

The drunk scratches his head and says, "Dang, I must be. The last two places said the same thing."

Let's Get Started!

A drunk was in front of a judge. The judge says, "You've been brought here for drinking."

The drunk says, "Okay, let's get started."

Drunk or Deaf?

A drunk is driving through the city and his car is weaving violently all over the road. A cop pulls him over and asks, "Where have you been?"

"I've been to the pub," slurs the drunk.

"Well," says the cop, "it looks like you've had quite a few."

"Did you know," says the cop, standing straight and folding his arms, "that a few intersections back, your wife fell out of your car?"

"Oh, thank heavens," sighs the drunk. "For a minute there, I thought I'd gone deaf."

CHAPTER TWO

THE GOOD OL' USA

Bob Hope once said that the United States has the best government money can buy.

Will Rogers added, "Be thankful we're not getting all the government we're paying for."

And Mark Twain famously commented, "Suppose you were an idiot... And suppose you were a member of Congress ... But I repeat myself."

Here in the good ol' USA, we have plenty of ironies, which brings to mind all those funny 'Only in America' jokes:

Only In America...

Only in America....do we use the word 'politics' to describe the process so well: 'Poli' in Latin meaning 'many' and 'tics' meaning 'bloodsucking creatures.'

Only in America...can a pizza get to your house faster than an ambulance.

Only in America...do banks leave both doors open and then chain the pens to the counters.

Only in America...are there handicap parking places in front of a skating rink.

Only in America...do we have drive-up ATM machines with Braille lettering.

Only in America...do drugstores make the sick walk all the way to the back of the store to get their prescriptions while healthy people can buy cigarettes at the front.

Only in America...do we leave cars worth thousands of dollars in the driveway and put our useless junk in the garage.

Only in America...do we use answering machines to screen calls and then have call waiting so we won't miss a call from someone we didn't want to talk to in the first place.

Only in America...could politicians talk about the greed of the rich at a $35,000 a plate campaign fund raising event.

Only in America...do we trample others for sales on Black Friday exactly one day after being thankful for what we already have.

Only in America...do we yell for speed laws that will stop fast driving, then won't buy a car if it can't go over 100 miles an hour.

Only in America... do we talk about baseball, shopping or fishing at the office, but when we are out at the game, the mall, or on the lake, we talk about business.

Only in America...do we have more food to eat than any other country in the world and more diets to keep us from eating it.

Only in Pennsylvania...

The following are a few jokes in honor of my home state, Pennsylvania, where every highway eventually narrows to a single lane and our two seasons include winter and construction:

You know you're from Pennsylvania if...

- The first day of buck season and the first day of doe season are school holidays.
- You can use the phrase "fire hall wedding reception" and not even bat an eye.
- At least five people on your block have electric "candles" in all or most of their windows all year long.
- You know what a "Hex sign" is.
- Words like hoagie, crick, chipped ham, sticky buns, shoo-fly pie, and pierogies actually mean something to you.
- You have not only heard of Birch Beer, but you know it comes in several colors: red, white, brown, and gold.
- You know several places to purchase or that serve Scrapple, Summer Sausage (Lebanon Bologna), and Hot Bacon Dressing.
- You know the difference between a cheese steak, a pizza steak sandwich, and a Primanti's, and know that you can't get a really good one outside of Pennsylvania.
- You live for summer, when street and county fairs signal the beginning of funnel cake season.
- Customers ask the waitress for "drippy eggs" for breakfast.
- You know what a township, borough, and commonwealth is.

- A traffic jam is 10 cars waiting to pass a horse-drawn carriage on the highway in Lancaster County.
- You know several people who have hit deer more than once.
- You carry jumper cables in your car and your female passengers know how to use them.
- Driving is always better in winter because the potholes are filled with snow.
- You learned to pronounce Bryn Mawr, Wilkes-Barre, Schuylkill, Bala Cynwyd, Conshohocken, and Monongahela.
- You know what a "Mummer" is, and are disappointed if you can't catch at least highlights of the parade.
- You actually understand these jokes and send him on to other Pennsylvanians.

Only in California...

In honor of the state where I have a second home and often visit, I offer up the following California jokes:

You know you're from California if...

- You drive to your neighborhood block party.
- Your coworker has eight body piercings and none are visible.
- You make over $300,000 a year and still can't afford a house.
- Your child's third-grade teacher has purple hair, a nose ring, and is named Breeze.
- You can't remember... is pot illegal?

- A really great parking space can totally move you to tears.
- It's barely sprinkling and there's a report on every news station: "STORM WATCH 2014."
- You know how to eat an artichoke.
- You can't remember... is pot illegal?
- The fastest part of your commute is going down the driveway.
- Your hairdresser is straight, your plumber is gay, the woman who delivers your mail is into S & M, and your Mary Kay rep is a guy in drag.
- Your car insurance costs as much as your house payment.
- Hey!!! Is pot illegal???

And just so the rest of the country doesn't feel left out...

Only In Texas...

A TEXAN'S GUIDE TO LIFE

1. Don't squat with your spurs on.
2. Never kick a cow chip on a hot day.
3. Never slap a man who's chewing tobacco.
4. When you give a lesson in meanness to a critter or a person, don't be surprised if they learn their lesson.
5. There are three kinds of men: The one that learns by reading, the few who learn by observation, and the rest of them who have to pee on the electric fence for themselves.

Only In Alaska...

You know you're from Alaska if:

- You know which leaves make good toilet paper.
- You know the four seasons: Winter, Still Winter, Almost Winter, and Construction
- You have to put your sun visor down at 3:00 a.m.
- All of your relatives refer to you as that crazy person that lives up there.
- The mosquitoes have landing lights.
- You have more miles on your snow blower than your car.
- You have 10 favorite recipes for moose meat.
- Your bedroom windows are covered in aluminum foil.
- You have worn a tie with waders.
- Sexy lingerie is anything flannel with less than eight buttons.
- The most effective mosquito repellent is a shotgun.

Only in Arizona...

You know you're from Arizona if:

- You learn that a seat belt makes a pretty good branding iron.
- The best parking place is determined by shade not distance.
- The temperature drops below 95 degrees and you feel a bit chilly.
- It's noon in July, kids are on summer vacation, and not one person is out on the streets.

Only in Hawaii...

You know you're from Hawaii if:

- You use your open car door for a dressing room.
- Your only suit is a bathing suit.
- You drive barefoot.
- You can live and let live with a smile in your heart.
- You call everyone older than yourself "Aunty" or "Uncle" and kiss everyone in greeting and farewell.

Only In New York...

You know you live in New York if:

- You think Central Park is "nature."
- You believe that being able to swear at people in their own language makes you multilingual.
- You've worn out a car horn.
- You say "the city" and expect everyone to know you mean Manhattan.
- You can get into a four hour argument about how to get from Columbus Circle to Battery Park, but can't find Wisconsin on a map.
- You have never been to the Statue of Liberty.

Only in the Deep South...

You know you live in the south if:

- You can rent a movie and buy bait in the same store.
- "Ya'll" is considered singular and "all ya'll" is plural.
- After 15 years, you still hear, "You're ain't from around here, are ya?"
- Everyone has two first names.

Only in Colorado...

You know you're from Colorado if:

- You carry a $3000 bicycle on top of your $500 car.
- The top of your head is bald but you still wear a ponytail.
- You think the major food groups are granola bars, tofu, and Fat Tire Beer.
- A pass does not involve a football or dating.

Only in the Midwest...

You know you live in the Midwest if:

- Your idea of a traffic jam is 10 cars waiting to pass a tractor.
- You end sentences with the question: "Where's my coat?"
- You've switched from Heat to A/C on the same day.
- You've never met any celebrities, but the mayor knows your name.

Only in Florida...

You're from Florida if;

- Cars in front of you are often driven by headless people.
- You eat dinner at 3:15 in the afternoon.
- Everyone can recommend a good dermatologist.
- All purchases include a coupon of some kind – even houses and cars.

Buy American Products

Regarding job layoffs in the U.S.:

Joe Smith started the day early having set his alarm clock (MADE IN JAPAN) for 6 a.m. While his coffeepot (MADE IN CHINA) was perking, he shaved with his electric razor (MADE IN HONG KONG). He put on a dress shirt (MADE IN SRI LANKA), designer jeans (MADE IN SINGAPORE) and tennis shoes (MADE IN KOREA).

After cooking his breakfast in his new electric skillet (MADE IN INDIA) he sat down with his calculator (MADE IN MEXICO) to see how much he could spend today. After setting his watch (MADE IN TAIWAN) to the radio (MADE IN INDIA) he got in his car (MADE IN GERMANY) and continued his search for a good paying AMERICAN JOB.

At the end of yet another discouraging and fruitless day, Joe decided to relax for a while. He put on his sandals (MADE IN BRAZIL) poured himself a glass of wine (MADE IN FRANCE) and turned on his TV (MADE IN INDONESIA), and then wondered why he can't find a good paying job in.....AMERICA!

Old Geezers and the Military

I'm over 50 now and the Armed Forces say I'm too old to track down terrorists. You can't be older than 35 to join the military.

They've got the whole thing backwards. Instead of sending 18-year-olds off to fight, they ought to take us old guys. You shouldn't be able to join until you're at least 35.

For starters: Researchers say 18-year-olds think about sex every 10 seconds. Old guys only think about sex a couple of times a day, leaving us more than 28,000 additional seconds per day to concentrate on the enemy.

Young guys haven't lived long enough to be cranky, and a cranky soldier is a dangerous soldier.

If we can't kill the enemy we'll complain them into submission. "My back hurts!" "I'm hungry!" "Where's the remote control?"

An 18-year-old hasn't had a legal beer yet and you shouldn't go to war until you're at least old enough to legally drink. An average old guy, on the other hand, has consumed 126,000 gallons of beer by the time he's 35 and a jaunt through the desert heat with a backpack and M-60 would do wonders for the old beer belly.

An 18-year-old doesn't like to get up before 10 a.m. Old guys get up early (to pee).

If old guys are captured, we couldn't spill the beans because we'd probably forgot where we put them. In fact, name, rank, and serial number would be a real brainteaser.

Boot camp would actually be easier for old guys. We're used to getting screamed and yelled at and we actually like soft food. We've also developed a deep appreciation for guns and rifles. We like them almost better than naps.

They could lighten up on the obstacle course, however. I've been in combat and didn't see a single 20-foot wall with rope hanging over the side, nor did I ever do any pushups after training. I can hear the Drill Sergeant now, "Get down and give me...er...one."

And the running part is kind of a waste of energy. I've never seen anyone outrun a bullet.

An 18-year-old has the whole world ahead of him. He's still learning to shave, to actually carry on a conversation, to wear pants without the top of the butt crack showing and the boxer shorts sticking out, to learn that a pierced tongue catches food particles, and that a 200-watt speaker in the back seat of a Honda Accord can rupture an eardrum.

All great reasons to keep our sons at home and to learn a little more about life before sending them off to a possible death. Let us old guys track down those dirty rotten terrorists. The last thing the enemy would want to see right now is a couple of million old farts with attitudes.

CHAPTER THREE

MARRIAGE — FOR BETTER OR WORSE

This following section is dedicated to the memory of the old Jewish Catskill comics from Vaudeville days.

Here are some of their famous comedic lines about marriage:

Some Vaudeville Humor...

My wife and I went to a hotel where we got a waterbed. My wife called it the Dead Sea.

Q: Why are Jewish men circumcised?
A: Because Jewish women don't like anything that isn't 20% off.

I've been in love with the same woman for 49 years. If my wife ever finds out, she'll kill me!

What are three words a woman never wants to hear when she's making love? "Honey, I'm home."

Someone stole all my credit cards, but I won't be reporting it. The thief spends less than my wife does.

We always hold hands. If I let go, she shops.

I was just in London. There is a six-hour time difference. I'm still confused. When I go to dinner, I feel sexy. When I go to bed, I feel hungry.

There was a girl knocking on my hotel room door all night! Finally, I let her out.

Why do Jewish divorces cost so much? They're worth it.

Why do Jewish men die before their wives? They want to.

The Harvard School of Medicine did a study of why Jewish women like Chinese food so much. The study revealed that this is due to the fact that Won Ton spelled backward is Not Now.

I just got back from a pleasure trip. I took my mother-in-law to the airport.

Top 10 Reasons Why Some Men Favor Handguns Over Women

#10   You can trade an old 44 for a new 22.

#9   You can keep one handgun at home and have another for when you're on the road.

#8   If you admire a friend's handgun and tell him so, he will probably let you try it out a few times.

#7   Your primary handgun doesn't mind if you keep another handgun for a backup.

#6   Your handgun will stay with you even if you run out of ammo.

#5   A handgun doesn't take up a lot of closet space.

#4   Handguns function normally every day of the month.

#3   A handgun doesn't ask, "Do these new grips make me look fat?"

#2   A handgun doesn't mind if you go to sleep after you use it.

And the number one reason a handgun is favored over a woman:

#1   You can buy a silencer for a handgun.

Where is Larry's Bar?

A man goes to a shrink and says, "Doctor, my wife is unfaithful to me. Every evening, she goes to Larry's bar and picks up men. In fact, she sleeps with anybody who asks her! I'm going crazy. What do you think I should do?"

"Relax," says the Doctor. "Take a deep breath and calm down. Now, tell me, exactly where is Larry's bar?"

The Curse

An old man goes to the Wizard to ask him if he can remove a curse he has been living with for the last 40 years.

The Wizard says, "Okay, but you will have to tell me the exact words that were used to put the curse on you."

The old man answers without hesitation, "I now pronounce you man and wife."

Brewing Coffee

A man and his wife were having an argument about who should brew the coffee each morning.

The wife says, "You should do it, because you get up first, and then we don't have to wait as long to get our coffee."

"You are in charge of the cooking around here and you should do it, because that is your job, and I can just wait for my coffee," the husband argues.

"No, you should do it," the wife insists. "It says in the Bible that the man should do the coffee."

"I can't believe that. Show me."

So the wife fetches the Bible and opens the New Testament and shows him at the top of several pages that it does, indeed, say: "HEBREWS."

The Blue Pill

A woman asks her husband if he'd like some breakfast. "Would you like bacon and eggs perhaps, or maybe a slice of toast and some grapefruit and coffee?"

He declines. "It's this Viagra," he says. "It's really taken the edge off my appetite."

At lunchtime, she asks if he would like something. "A bowl of homemade soup, homemade muffins, or a ham and cheese sandwich?" she inquires.

He declines. "Still not hungry," he says. "The Viagra really trashes my desire for food."
Come dinnertime, she asks him if he wants anything to eat. Would he like maybe a steak and apple pie? Maybe he'd like a microwave pizza or a tasty stir-fry that would only take a couple of minutes?

He declines. "Nah, still not hungry."

"Well," she says, "would you mind letting me up? I'm starving."

Make a Wish

A man walking along a California beach was deep in prayer. Suddenly, the sky clouded above his head and the Lord said in a booming voice, "Because you have tried to be faithful to me in all ways, I will grant you one wish."

The man said, "Build a bridge to Hawaii so I can drive over anytime I want."

The Lord said, "Your request is very materialistic. Think of the enormous challenges for that kind of undertaking. The supports required to reach the bottom of the Pacific! The concrete and steel it would take! It will nearly exhaust several natural resources. I can do it, but it is hard for me to justify your desire for worldly things. Take a little more time and think of something that would honor and glorify me."

The man thought about it for a long time. Finally, he said, "Lord, I wish that I could understand my wife. I want to know what she feels inside, what she's thinking when she gives me the silent treatment, why she cries, what she means when she says 'nothing is wrong,' and how I can make a woman truly happy."

The Lord replied, "You want that bridge two or four lanes?"

By His Side

This woman's husband had been slipping in and out of a coma for several months, yet she had stayed by his bedside every single day. One day, when he came to, he motioned for her to come nearer.

As she sat by him, he whispered, eyes full of tears, "You know what? You have been with me through all the bad times. When I got fired, you were there to support me. When my business failed, you were there. When I got shot, you were by my side.

When we lost the house, you stayed right here. When my health started failing, you were still by my side. You know what?"

"What, dear?" she gently asked, smiling as her heart began to fill with warmth.

"I think you're bad luck."

Humor in the Face of Defeat

The ultimate response to a Dear John letter:

A Marine was deployed to Afghanistan. While he was there, he received a letter from his girlfriend. In the letter, she explained that she had slept with two guys while he had been gone and she wanted to break up with him. AND she wanted pictures of herself back.

So, the Marine did what any squared-away Marine would do. He went around to his buddies and collected all the unwanted photos of women he could find. He then mailed about 25 pictures of women (with clothes and without) to his girlfriend with the following note: "I don't remember which one you are. Please remove your picture and send the rest back."

Bada-Bing, Bada-Boom

Three men were sitting together bragging about how they had set their recent brides straight on their duties.

The first man had married a woman from California and bragged that he had told his wife she was going to do all the dishes and house cleaning that needed to be done at their house. He said that it took a couple days, but on the third day he came home to a clean house and the dishes were all washed and put away.

The second man had married a woman from Ohio. He bragged to the guys that he had given his new bride orders that she was to do all the cleaning, dishes, and cooking. He told them that the first day he didn't see any results, but the next day it was better. By the third day, his house was clean, the dishes were done and he had come home to a huge dinner on the table.

The third man had married a Jersey girl. He boasted to the guys that he told her his house was to be cleaned, the dishes washed, the cooking done, and the laundry washed and ironed and this was all her responsibility. He said the first day he didn't see anything and the second day he didn't see anything, but by the third day, some of the swelling had gone down so he could see a little out of his left eye.

Wrinkles and Crinkles

A husband walks into Fredericks of Hollywood to purchase some sheer lingerie for his wife. He is shown several possibilities that range from $250 to $500 in price. The sheerer the lingerie was, the higher the price.

He opts for the sheerest item, pays the $500, and takes the lingerie home. He presents it to his wife and asks her to go upstairs, put it on, and model it for him.

Upstairs, the wife thinks, I have an idea. It's so sheer that it might as well be nothing. I'll not put it on, do the modeling naked, and return it to the store tomorrow and get a $500 refund for myself.

So she appears naked on the balcony and strikes a pose.

The husband says, "Good Lord! You'd think that for $500, they'd at least iron it!"

Tell Me Something Good

A husband and wife are getting ready for bed. The wife is standing in front of a full-length mirror taking a hard look at herself.

"You know, dear," she says, "I look in the mirror, and I see an old woman. My face is all wrinkled, my boobs are barely above my waist, and my butt is hanging out a mile. I've got fat legs and my arms are all flabby."

She turns to her husband and says, "Tell me something positive to make me feel better about myself."

He thinks about it for a bit and then says in a soft, thoughtful voice, "Well, there's nothing wrong with your eyesight."

Services will be held Saturday at St. Pat's Memorial Chapel.

What Do Women Want?

Young King Arthur was ambushed and imprisoned by the monarch of a neighboring kingdom. The monarch could have killed him but was moved by Arthur's youth and ideals. So the monarch offered him his freedom as long as he could answer a very difficult question. Arthur would have a year to figure out the answer and, if after a year, he still had no answer, he would be put to death.

The question: What do women really want?

Such a question would perplex even the most knowledgeable man, and to young Arthur, it seemed an impossible query. But, since it was better than death, he accepted the monarch's proposition to have an answer by year's end.

He returned to his kingdom and began to poll everyone: the princess, the priests, the wise men, and even the court jester. He spoke with everyone, but no one could give him a satisfactory answer.

Many people advised him to consult the old witch, for only she would have the answer. But the price would be high; as the witch was famous throughout the kingdom for the exorbitant prices she charged.

The last day of the year arrived and Arthur had no choice but to talk to the witch. She agreed to answer the question, but he would have to agree to her price first. The old witch wanted to marry Sir Lancelot, the most noble of the Knights of the Round Table and Arthur's closest friend!

Young Arthur was horrified. She was hunched backed and hideous, had only one tooth, smelled like sewage, and made obscene noises. He had never encountered such a repugnant creature in all his life. He refused to force his friend to marry her and endure such a terrible burden, but Lancelot, learning of the proposal, spoke with Arthur. He said nothing was too big of a sacrifice compared to Arthur's life and the preservation of the Round Table.

Hence, a wedding was proclaimed and the witch answered Arthur's question thus: "What a woman really wants," she answered, "is to be in charge of her own life."

Everyone in the kingdom instantly knew that the witch had uttered a great truth and that Arthur's life would be spared.

And so it was, the neighboring monarch granted Arthur his freedom and Lancelot and the witch had a wonderful wedding. The honeymoon hour approached and Lancelot, steeling himself for a horrific experience, entered the bedroom.

But, what a sight awaited him. The most beautiful woman he had ever seen lay before him on the bed. The astounded Lancelot asked what had happened. The beauty replied that since he had been so kind to her when she appeared as a witch, she would henceforth be her horrible deformed self only half the time and the beautiful maiden the other half. Which would he prefer? Beautiful during the day or night?

Lancelot pondered the predicament. During the day, he could have a beautiful woman to show off to his friends, but at night, in the privacy of his castle, he would have an old witch. Or, would he prefer having a hideous witch during the day, but by night, a beautiful woman for him to enjoy wondrous, intimate moments?

What would YOU do?

What Lancelot chose is below, BUT…. Make YOUR choice before you scroll down below, okay?

Nobel Lancelot, knowing the answer the witch gave Arthur to his question, said that he would allow HER to make the choice. Upon hearing this, she announced that she would be beautiful all the time because he had respected her enough to let her be in charge of her own life.

Now… what's the moral of the story?

The moral is: If you don't let a woman have her own way, things are going to get ugly.

A Night at the Strip Club

A wife decides to take her husband to a strip club for his birthday.

They arrive at the club and the doorman says, "Hey, Dave! How are you doing?" His wife is puzzled and asks if he's been to this club before. "Oh no," says Dave. "He's on my bowling team."

When they are seated, a waitress asks Dave if he'd like his usual and brings over a Budweiser. His wife is becoming increasingly uncomfortable and asks, "How did she know that you drink Budweiser?"

"She's in the Ladies' Bowling League, honey," he explains. "We share lanes with them."

A stripper then comes over to their table, throws her arms around Dave, and says "Hi Davey. Want your usual table dance, big boy?"

Dave's wife, now furious, grabs her purse and storms out of the club. Dave follows and spots her getting into a cab. Before she can slam the door, he jumps in beside her. He tries desperately to explain how the stripper must have mistaken him for someone else, but his wife is having none of it. She is screaming at him at the top of her lungs, calling him every name in the book.

The cabby turns his head and says, "Looks like you picked up a real bitch tonight, Dave."

Mules, Goats, and Pigs

A couple drove down a country road for several miles, not saying a word. An earlier discussion had led to an argument and neither of them wanted to concede their position.

As they passed a barnyard of mules, goats, and pigs, his wife asked sarcastically, "Relatives of yours?"

"Yup," the husband replied. "In-laws."

A Lesson in Assertiveness

I was tired of being bossed around by my wife; so I went to a psychiatrist.

The psychiatrist said I needed to build my self-esteem, and so he gave me a book on assertiveness, which I read on the way home. I finished the book by the time I reached my house. I stormed into the house and walked up to my wife.

Pointing a finger in her face, I said, "From now on, I want you to know that I am the man of this house and my word is law! I want you to prepare me a gourmet meal tonight and when I'm finished eating my meal, I expect a sumptuous dessert afterwards. Then, after dinner, you're going to draw me my bath so I can relax. And, when I'm finished with my bath, guess who's going to dress me and comb my hair?"

"The funeral director," she said.

What?

A husband read an article to his wife about how many words women use a day... 30,000 to a man's 15,000 words.

The wife replied, "The reason has to be because a woman has to say everything twice."

The husband then turned to his wife and asked, "What?"

Let Me Explain

A man said to his wife one day, "I don't know how you can be so stupid and beautiful all at the same time."

The wife responded, "Allow me to explain it to you. God made me beautiful so you would be attracted to me; God made me stupid so I would be attracted to you."

Women's Humor

One day, my housework-challenged husband decided to wash his sweatshirt.

Seconds after he stepped into the laundry room, he shouted to me, "What setting do I use on the washing machine?"

"It depends," I replied. "What does it say on your shirt?"

He yelled back, "University of Oklahoma."

And they say blondes are dumb.

Gotta Love That Fairy!

A man and his wife, now in their 60's, were celebrating their 40th wedding anniversary. On their special day, a good fairy came to them and said that because they had been such a devoted couple she would grant each of them a very special wish.

The wife wished for a trip around the world with her husband. Whoosh! Immediately she had airline/cruise tickets in her hands.

The man wished for a female companion 30 years younger. Whoosh! Immediately he turned 90!

Make My Day

A couple is lying in bed.

The man says, "I am going to make you the happiest woman in the world."

The woman says, "I'll miss you."

A Prayer...

Dear Lord, I pray for wisdom to understand my man; love to forgive him; and patience for his moods.

Because, Lord, if I pray for strength, I'll beat him to death.

Words to the Wise

HOW TO IMPRESS A WOMAN:

Wine her, dine her, call her, hug her, support her, hold her, surprise her, compliment her, smile at her, listen to her, laugh with her, cry with her, romance her, encourage her, believe in her, pray with her, pray for her, cuddle with her, shop with her, give her jewelry, buy her flowers, hold her hand, and write love letters to her. Go to the end of the earth and back again for her.

HOW TO IMPRESS A MAN:

Show up naked, bring chicken wings, and don't block the TV.

Dining Out

A man and his wife are seated in a fancy French restaurant for dinner.

When the waiter arrives at their table, the man says, "I'll have your biggest, thickest, rawest Porterhouse steak."

His waiter replies, "What about mad cow?"

The man replies, "She'll have a salad."

CHAPTER FOUR

ROCK OF AGES

What's so funny about getting old? Turns out – plenty!

The Doctor Says...

The doctor gave a man six months to live. The man couldn't pay his bill, so he gave him another six months.

The doctor called Mrs. Cohen saying, "Mrs. Cohen, your check came back." Mrs. Cohen answered, "So did my arthritis!"

The doctor tells his patient, "You'll live to be 60!" The patient replies impatiently, "I AM 60." The doctor says, "See, what did I tell you?"

A doctor has a stethoscope up to a man's chest. The man asks "Doc, how do I stand?" The doctor says "That's what puzzles me!"

"Doctor, I have a ringing in my ears," an elderly patient complains. "Don't answer!" the doctor answers.

An elderly man went to his doctor and said, "Doc, I think I'm getting senile. Several times lately, I have forgotten to zip up." "That's not senility," replied the doctor. "Senility is when you forget to zip down."

Getting Old

George, a 70-year-old grandfather, went for his annual physical. All of his tests came back with normal results.

Dr. Smith said, "George, everything looks great physically. How are you doing mentally and emotionally? Are you at peace with yourself? Do you have a good relationship with your God?"

George replied, "God and me are tight. He knows I have poor eyesight, so he's fixed it so that when I get up in the middle of the night to go to the bathroom, poof! The light goes on when I pee. And then, poof! The light goes off when I'm done."

"Wow," commented Dr. Smith, "that's incredible!"

A little later in the day Dr. Smith called George's wife. "Thelma," he said, "George is just fine. Physically, he's great. But I had to call because I'm in awe of his relationship with God. Is it true that he gets up during the night and, poof, the light goes on in the bathroom, and then, poof, the light goes off?"

Thelma exclaimed, "That old fool! He's peeing in the refrigerator again!"

Ramblings of a Retired Mind

I was thinking that women should put pictures of missing husbands on beer cans!

I was thinking about how a status symbol of today is those cell phones that everyone has clipped on. Since I can't afford one, I'm wearing my garage door opener.

You know, I spent a fortune on deodorant before I realized that people didn't like me anyway.

I was thinking about old age and decided that it is when you still have something on the ball but you are just too tired to bounce it.

I thought about making a fitness movie for folks my age and calling it: Pumping Rust.

I have gotten that dreaded furniture disease. That's when your chest is falling into your drawers.

Employment applications always ask who is to be notified in case of an emergency. I think you should write, "A good doctor!"

I was thinking about how people seem to read the Bible a whole lot more as they get older," George Carlin joked. "Then it dawned on me – they're cramming for their final exam."

Social Security Application

A retired man went to apply for Social Security. After waiting in line for a long time, he got to the counter. The woman asked him for his driver's license to verify his age. He looked in his pockets and realized that he left his wallet at home. He told the woman that he was very sorry. "I will have to go home and get my wallet and come back later," he explained.

The woman said, "Unbutton your shirt." So he opened his shirt revealing lots of curly silver hair. She said, "That silver hair on your chest is proof enough for me," and processed his Social Security application.

When he got home, the man excitedly told his wife about his experience at the Social Security office.

She said "You should have dropped your pants; you might have gotten disability, too."

In Defense of Senior Citizens

Senior citizens are constantly being criticized for every conceivable deficiency of the modern world – real or imaginary. We take responsibility for all we have done and do not blame others.

However, upon reflection, we would like to point out that it was NOT senior citizens who took:

- The melody out of music,
- The pride out of appearance,
- The courtesy out of driving,
- The romance out of love,
- The commitment out of marriage,
- The responsibility out of parenthood,
- The togetherness out of family,
- The learning out of education,
- The service out of patriotism,
- The Golden Rule from rulers,

- The nativity scene out of cities,
- The civility out of behavior,
- The refinement out of language,
- The dedication out of employment,
- The prudence out of spending,
- The ambition out of achievement, or,
- God out of government and school.

And we certainly are NOT the ones who eliminated patience and tolerance from personal relationships and interactions with others.

And, we do understand the meaning of patriotism, and remember those who have fought and died for our country.

Does anyone under the age of 50 know the lyrics to the Star Spangled Banner? What about the last verse of My Country 'tis of Thee? "Our father's God to thee, author of liberty, To Thee we sing. Long may our land be bright, With freedom's Holy light. Protect us by Thy might, Great God our King."

Just look at the seniors with tears in their eyes and pride in their hearts as they stand at attention with their hand over their hearts!

Yes, I'm a Senior Citizen!

- I'm the life of the party... even if it lasts until 8 p.m.
- I'm very good at opening childproof caps... with a hammer.
- I'm usually interested in going home before I get to where I am going.
- I'm awake many hours before my body allows me to get up.
- I'm smiling all the time because I can't hear a thing you're saying.

- I'm very good at telling stories; over and over and over and over…
- I'm aware that other people's grandchildren are not nearly as cute as mine.
- I'm so cared for—long term care, eye care, private care, dental care.
- I'm not really grouchy. I just don't like traffic, waiting, crowds, lawyers, loud music, and a few other things I can't seem to remember right now.
- I'm sure everything I can't find is in a safe and secure place…somewhere.
- I'm wrinkled, saggy, lumpy, and that's just my left leg.
- I'm having trouble remembering simple words like…
- I'm beginning to realize that aging is not for wimps.
- I'm sure they are making adults much younger these days and when did they let kids become policemen?
- I was wondering…if you're only as old as you feel, how could I be alive at 150?
- And, how can my kids be older than I feel sometimes?
- I'm a walking storeroom of facts. I've just lost the key to the storeroom door.
- Yes, I'm a SENIOR CITIZEN and I think I am having the time of my life!
- Now if I could only remember who sent this to me, I wouldn't send it back to them, but I would send it to many more!
- Have I already sent this to you?
- If so, I'll try not to do it again (for a while).

Gasmen

Two gas company servicemen, a senior training supervisor, and a young trainee were out checking meters in a suburban neighborhood. They parked their truck at the end of the alley and worked their way to the other end.

At the last house, a woman looking out her kitchen window watched as they checked her meter.

Finishing the meter check, the senior supervisor challenged his younger co-worker to a footrace down the alley and back to the truck to prove that an older guy could outrun a younger one.

As they came tearing up to the truck, they realized the lady from the last house was huffing and puffing right behind them. They stopped immediately and asked her what was wrong.

"When I saw two gasmen running as hard as you were," gasped the woman, "I figured I'd better run too!"

We Used To...

We used to go out dining and couldn't get our fill.
Now we ask for doggie bags, come home, and take a pill.

We used to go to weddings, football games, and brunches.
Now we go to funeral homes, and after-funeral brunches.

We used to often travel to places near and far.
Now we get sore butts from riding in the car.

We used to go out shopping for new clothing at the mall. Now we never bother... all the sizes are too small.

We used to go to nightclubs and drink a little booze.
Now we stay at home at night and watch the evening news.

That, my friend is how life is and now my tale is told.

So, enjoy each day and live it up... before you get too old!

Gifts for Mama

Four brothers left home for college and became successful doctors and lawyers and prospered. Years later, they were chatting after having dinner together.

They discussed the gifts that they were able to give to their elderly mother, who lived far away in another city.

The first said, "I had a big house built for mama."

The second said, "I had a hundred thousand dollar theater built in the house."

The third said, "I had my Mercedes dealer deliver her an SL600 with a chauffeur."

The fourth said, "Listen to this. You know how mama loved reading the Bible and you know she can't read it anymore because she can't see very well. I met this monk who told me about a parrot that can recite the entire Bible. It took 20 monks 12 years to teach him. I had to pledge them $100,000.00 a year for 20 years to the church, but it was worth it. Mama just has to name the chapter and verse and the parrot will recite it."

The other brothers were impressed. After the holidays Mama sent out thank-you notes.

She wrote: Dear Milton, the house you built is so huge. I live in only one room, but I have to clean the whole house. Thanks anyways.

Dear Mike, you gave me an expensive theater with Dolby sound that could hold 50 people. But all my friends are dead, I've lost my hearing, and I'm nearly blind. I'll never use it. But thank-you for the gesture just the same.

Dear Marvin, I am too old to travel. I stay home, I have my groceries delivered, so I never use the Mercedes... and the driver you hired is a big jerk. But the thought was good. Thanks.

Dearest Melvin, you were the only son to have the good sense to give a little thought to your gift. The chicken was delicious. Thank-you.

I Know this Alphabet Well

A is for arthritis,
B is for bad back,
C is for chest pains. Perhaps cardiac?
D is for dental decay and decline,
E is for eyesight—can't read that top line.
F is for fissures and fluid retention.
G is for gas (which I'd rather not mention).
H is for high blood pressure (I'd rather have low).
I is for incisions with scars you can show.
J is for joints that now fail to flex.
L is for libido—what happened to sex?
K is for my knees that crack when they're bent.
(Please forgive me, my **M**emory ain't worth a cent).
N is for neurosis, pinched nerves and stiff neck,
O is for osteo-and all bones that crack,
P is for prescription, I have quite a few.
Q is for queasiness. Fatal or flu?
R is for reflux—one meal turns into two.
S is for sleepless nights, counting my fears.

T is for tinnitus—I hear bells in my ears.
U is for urinary: difficulties with flow.
V is for vertigo, that's "dizzy", you know.
W is worry, now what's going 'round?
X is for X ray—and what might be found.
Y is for another year I've left behind.
Z is for zest that I still have my mind.

I have survived all the symptoms my body's deployed, and kept twenty-six doctor gainfully employed!

Aches and Pains

A little old man shuffled slooowwwly into an ice cream parlor, pulled himself very slooowwwly and painfully up onto a chair. After catching his breath, he ordered a banana split.

His waitress asked kindly, "Crushed nuts?"

"No," he replied, "Arthritis."

Christmas Day Golf

Four old timers were playing their weekly game of golf. One remarked how for Christmas this year he'd love to wake up on Christmas morning, roll out of bed and, without an argument, go directly to the golf course, meet his buddies, and play a round.

His buddies all chimed in and said, "Let's do it! We'll make it a priority, figure out a way and meet here early, Christmas morning."

Months later, that special morning arrives, and there they are on the golf course.

The first guy says, "Boy this game cost me a fortune! I bought my wife such a diamond ring that she can't take her eyes off it."

Number 2 guy says, "I spent a ton too. My wife is at home planning the cruise I gave her. She was up to her eyeballs in brochures."

Number 3 guy says, "Well, my wife is at home admiring her new car, reading the manual."

They all turned to the last guy in the group and he is staring at them like they have lost their minds.

"I can't believe you all went to such expense for this golf game. I slapped my wife on the butt and said, 'Well babe, is it sex or golf?' She said, 'Take a sweater.'"

I Can Hear Just Fine

Three retirees, each with a hearing loss, were playing golf one fine March day.

One remarked to the other, "Windy, isn't it?"

"No," the second man replied, "it's Thursday."

And the third man chimed in, "So am I. Let's have a beer."

Soup or Sex

A little old lady was running up and down the halls in a nursing home. As she walked, she would flip up the hem of her nightgown and say, "Super sex."

She walked up to an elderly man in a wheelchair. Flipping her gown at him, she said, "Super sex."

He sat silently for a moment or two and finally answered "I'll take the soup."

Romance

An older couple were lying in bed one night. The husband was falling asleep but the wife was in a romantic mood and wanted to talk.

She said: "You used to hold my hand when we were courting." Wearily he reached across, held her hand for a second, and then tried to get back to sleep.

A few moments later she said: "Then you used to kiss me." Mildly irritated, he reached across, gave her a peck on the cheek, and settled down to sleep.

Thirty seconds later, she said: "Then you used to bite my neck." Angrily, he threw back the bed clothes and got out of bed.

"Where are you going?" she asked.

"To get my teeth!"

Down at the Retirement Center

Eighty-year old Bessie bursts into the recreation room at the retirement home. She holds her clenched fist in the air and announces, "Anyone who can guess what's in my hand can have sex with me tonight!"

An elderly gentleman in the rear shouts out, "An elephant?"

Bessie thinks a minute and says, "Close enough."

Driving

Two elderly women were out driving in a large car. Both could barely see over the dashboard. As they were cruising along, they came to an intersection. The stoplight was red, but they just went on through.

The woman in the passenger seat thought to herself "I must be losing it. I could have sworn we just went through a red light."

After a few more minutes, they came to another intersection and the light was red again. Again, they went right through. The woman in the passenger seat was almost sure that the light had been red but was really concerned that she was losing it. She was getting nervous.

At the next intersection, sure enough, the light was red and they went on through. So, she turned to the other woman and said, "Mildred, did you know that we just ran through three red lights in a row? You could have killed us both!"

Mildred turned to her and said, "Crap, am I driving?"

Hunting Story

A 90-year-old man said to his doctor, "I've never felt better. I have an 18-year-old bride who is pregnant with my child. What do you think about that?"

The doctor considered his question for a minute and then said, "I have an elderly friend who is a hunter and never misses a season. One day, when he was going out in a bit of a hurry, he accidentally picked up his umbrella instead of his gun. When he got to the creek, he saw a beaver sitting beside the stream. He raised his umbrella and went, 'bang, bang' and the beaver fell dead. What do you think of that?"

The 90-year-old said, "I'd say somebody else shot that beaver."

The doctor replied, "My point exactly."

Getting Married

Jacob, age 92, and Rebecca, age 89, are all excited about their decision to get married. They go for a stroll to discuss the wedding and on the way they pass a drugstore. Jacob suggests they go in.

Jacob addresses the man behind the counter: "Are you the owner?"

The pharmacist answers, "Yes."

Jacob: "We're about to get married. Do you sell heart medication?"

Pharmacist: "Of course we do."

Jacob: "How about medicine for circulation?"

Pharmacist: "All kinds."

Jacob: "Medicine for rheumatism, scoliosis?"

Pharmacist: "Definitely."

Jacob: "How about Viagra?"

Pharmacist: "Of course."

Jacob: "Medicine for memory problems, arthritis, jaundice?"

Pharmacist: "Yes, a large variety. The works."

Jacob: "What about vitamins, sleeping pills, Geritol, antidotes for Parkinson's disease?"

Pharmacist: "Absolutely."

Jacob: "You sell wheelchairs and walkers?"

Pharmacist: "All speeds and sizes."

Jacob says to the Pharmacist: "We'd like to use this store as our Bridal Registry."

CHAPTER FIVE

HOLY SMOKE

The following is some religious humor that includes church, minister, and sermon jokes along with some cute Sunday school stories. Enjoy!

Church and Children

- After the christening of his baby brother in church, Jason sobbed all the way home in the back seat of the car. His father asked him three times what was wrong. Finally, the boy replied, "That preacher said he wanted us brought up in a Christian home and I wanted to stay with you guys."

- Three-year-old Reese prayed: "Our Father, Who does art in heaven, Harold is His name. Amen."

- A little boy was overheard praying: "Lord, if you can't make me a better boy, don't worry about it. I'm having a real good time like I am."

- A Sunday school class was studying the Ten Commandments. They were ready to discuss the last one. The teacher asked if anyone could tell her what it was. Susie raised her hand, stood tall, and quoted, "Thou shall not take the covers off the neighbor's wife."

- I had been teaching my three-year old daughter, Caitlin, the Lord's Prayer for several evenings at bedtime. She would repeat after me the lines from the prayer. Finally, she decided to go solo. I listened with pride as she carefully enunciated each word right up to the end of the prayer: "Lead us not into temptation," she prayed, "but deliver us some E-mail."

- A Sunday school teacher asked her class, "What was Jesus' mother's name?" One child answered, "Mary." The teacher then asked, "Who knows what Jesus' father's name was?" A little kid said, "Verge." Confused, the teacher asked, "Where did you get that?" The kid said, "Well, you know, they are always talking about Verge n' Mary."

- One four-year-old prayed, "And forgive us our trash baskets as we forgive those who put trash in our baskets."

- A Sunday school teacher asked her children, as they were on the way to church service, "And why is it necessary to be quiet in church?" One bright little girl replied, "Because people are sleeping."

- Six-year-old Angie and her four-year-old brother Joel were sitting together in church. Joel giggled, sang, and talked out loud. Finally, his big sister had had enough. "You're not supposed to talk out loud in church." "Why? Who's going to stop me?" Joel asked. Angie pointed to the back of the church and said, "See those two men standing by the door? They're hushers."

- A mother was preparing pancakes for her sons, Kevin, 5 and Ryan, 3. The boys began to argue over who would get the first pancake. Their mother saw the opportunity for a moral lesson. "If Jesus were sitting here, he would say, 'Let my brother have the first pancake, I can wait.'" Kevin turned to his younger brother and said, "Ryan, you be Jesus!"

- A father was at the beach with his children when his four-year-old son ran up to him, grabbed his hand, and led him to the shore where a seagull lay dead in the sand. "Daddy, what happened to him?" the son asked. "He died and went to Heaven," the Dad replied. The boy thought a moment and then said, "Did God throw him back down?"

- A wife invited some people to dinner. At the table, she turned to their six-year-old -daughter and said, "Would you like to say blessing?" "I wouldn't know what to say," the girl replied. "Just say what you hear Mommy say," the wife answered. The daughter bowed her head and said, "Lord, why on earth did I invite all these people to dinner?"

- A little girl was talking to her teacher about whales. The teacher said it was physically impossible for a whale to swallow a human because, even though it was a very large mammal, its throat was very small. The little girl stated that Jonah was swallowed by a whale. Irritated, the teacher reiterated that a whale could not swallow a human, it was physically impossible. The little girl said, "When I get to heaven I will ask Jonah." The teacher asked, "What if Jonah went to hell?" The little girl replied, "Then you ask him."

- A kindergarten teacher was observing her classroom of children while they were drawing. She would occasionally walk around to see each child's work. As she got to one little girl who was working diligently, she asked what the drawing was. The girl replied, "I'm drawing God." The teacher paused and said, "But no one knows what God looks like." Without missing a beat or looking up from her drawing, the girl replied, "They will in a minute."

- A Sunday school teacher was discussing the Ten Commandments with her five and six year olds. After explaining the commandment to "honor" thy Father and thy Mother, she asked, "Is there a commandment that teaches us how to treat our brothers and sisters?" One little boy (the oldest of a family) answered, "Thou shall not kill."

- The children were lined up in the cafeteria of a Catholic elementary school for lunch. At the head of the table was a large pile of apples. The nun made a note, and posted it on the apple tray: "Take only ONE. God is watching." Moving further along the lunch line, at the other end of the table was a large pile of chocolate chip cookies. A child had written a note, "Take all you want. God is watching the apples."

- A little boy riding on the bus sat next to a man reading a book and noticed he had his collar on backwards. The little boy asked why he wore his collar that way. The man, who was a priest, said, "I am a Father." The little boy replied, "My daddy doesn't wear his collar like that." The priest looked up from his book and answered "I am the

Father of many." The boy said, "My Dad has four boys, four girls and two grandchildren and he doesn't wear his collar that way." The priest, getting impatient, said, "I am the Father of hundreds." Then he went back to reading his book. The little boy sat quietly thinking for a while, then leaned over and said, "Maybe you should wear your pants backwards instead of your collar."

- A father was approached by his small son who told him proudly, "I know what the Bible means!" His father smiled and replied, "What do you mean, you 'know' what the Bible means?" The son replied, "I do know!" "Okay", said the father. "So, son, what does the Bible mean?" That's easy, Daddy. It stands for 'Basic Information Before Leaving Earth."

- Sunday after church, a mom asked her very young daughter what the lesson was about. The daughter answered, "Don't be scared, you'll get your quilt." Needless to say, the mom was perplexed. Later in the day, the pastor stopped by for tea and the Mom asked him what that morning's Sunday school lesson was about. He said, "Be not afraid, thy comforter is coming."

A Little Christian Humor

The best vitamin for a Christian is B1.

Don't give up. Moses was once a basket case.

To belittle is to be little.

God answers knee mail.

Never give the devil a ride. He will always want to drive.

Noah's Ark

Everything I need to know about life, I learned from Noah's Ark.

1. Don't miss the boat.
2. Remember that we are all in the same boat.
3. Plan ahead. It wasn't raining when Noah built the Ark.
4. Stay fit. When you're 600 years old, someone may ask you to do something really big.
5. Don't listen to critics; just get on with the job that needs to be done.
6. Build your future on high ground.
7. For safety sake, travel in pairs.
8. Speed isn't always an advantage. The snails were on board with the cheetahs.
9. When you're stressed, float a while.
10. Remember the Ark was built by amateurs; the Titanic by professionals.
11. No matter the storm, there's always a rainbow waiting.

Church Gossip

The church gossip and self-appointed arbiter of the church's morals, kept sticking her nose into other people's business.

Several church members were unappreciative of her activities, but feared her enough to maintain their silence. She made a mistake, however, when she accused George, a new member, of being drunk after she saw his pickup truck parked in front of the town's only bar one afternoon. She commented to George and others that everyone seeing it there would know what he was doing.

George, a man of few words, stared at her for a moment and just walked away. He didn't explain, defend, or deny; he said nothing.

Later that evening, George quietly parked his pickup in front of her house and left it there all night.

What People Want

People want the front of the bus, the back of the church, and the center of attention.

Anything Breakable?

There was a very gracious lady who was mailing an old family Bible to her brother in another part of the country. "Is there anything breakable in here?" asked the postal clerk. "Only the Ten Commandments." answered the lady.

Good Morning

Somebody has well said there are only two kinds of people in the world.

There are those who wake up in the morning and say, "Good morning, Lord."

And those who wake up in the morning and say, "Good Lord, it's morning."

Watch That Water

Three little boys were concerned because they couldn't get anyone to play with them. They decided it was because they had not been baptized and didn't go to Sunday school. So they went to the nearest church. Only the janitor was there.

One little boy said, "We need to be baptized because no one will come out and play with us. Will you baptize us?"

"Sure," said the janitor. He took them into the bathroom and dunked their little heads in the toilet bowl, one at a time. Then he said, "You are now baptized!"

When they got outside, one of them asked, "What religion do you think we are?"

The oldest one said, "We're not Kathlick...because they pour the water on you."

"We're not Babtis...because they dunk all of you in the water."

"We're not Methdiss...because they just sprinkle water on you."

The littlest one asked, "Didn't you smell that water?"

They all joined in asking, "Yeah! What do you think that means?"

"I think it means we're Pisscopailians."

Strange Diet

Two Irish nuns have just arrived in the USA by boat. One says to the other, "I hear that the people in this country actually eat dogs."

Nodding emphatically, the mother superior points to a hot dog vendor and they both walk towards the cart.

"Two dogs, please," says one.

The vendor is only too pleased to oblige and he wraps both hot dogs in foil and hands them over the counter.

Excited, the nuns hurry over to a bench and begin to unwrap their "dogs."

The mother superior is first to open hers. She begins to blush and then, staring at it for a moment, leans over to the other nun and whispers cautiously, "What part did you get?"

Quoting Scripture

A minister parked his car in a no-parking zone in a large city because he was short of time and couldn't find a space with a meter. Then he put a note under the windshield wiper that read: "I have circled the block 10 times. If I don't park here, I'll miss my appointment. Forgive us our trespasses."

When he returned, he found a citation from a police officer along with this note, "I've circled this block for 10 years. If I don't give you a ticket, I'll lose my job. Lead us not into temptation."

Good News and Bad News

There is the story of a pastor who got up one Sunday and announced to his congregation: "I have good news and bad news. The good news is that we have enough money to pay for your new building program. The bad news is that it's still out there in your pockets."

Confessions

Father O'Grady was saying his good-byes to the parishioners after his Sunday morning services as he always does, when Mary Clancey came up to him in tears.

"What's bothering you, dear?" asked Father O'Grady.

"Oh, Father, I've got terrible news," replied Mary. "My husband passed away last night."

"Oh, Mary!" said the good father. "That's terrible. Tell me, Mary, did he have any last requests?"

"Yes...," Mary replied sheepishly.

"Well?" "

"He said, 'Please, Mary, put down the gun!'"

Church Sign

A church sign wisely said, "You are never too bad to come in. You are never too good to stay out."

What a Deal

A Catholic priest was called away for an emergency.

Not wanting to leave the confessional unattended, he called his rabbi friend from across the street and asked him to cover for him. The rabbi told him he wouldn't know what to say, but the priest told him to come on over and he'd stay with him for a little bit and show him what to do.

The rabbi came and he and the priest went into the confessional. In a few minutes, a woman came in and said, "Father forgive me for I have sinned. I committed adultery."

The priest asked, "How many times?" The woman answered, "Three times."

The priest said, "Say two Hail Marys, put $5.00 in the box, and sin no more."

A few minutes later a man entered the confessional. He said, "Father forgive me for I have sinned."

The priest asked, "What did you do?" The man answered, "I committed adultery."

The priest asked, "How many times?" The man replied, "Three times."

The priest said, "Say two Hail Marys, put $5.00 in the box, and sin no more."

The Rabbi told the priest that he thought he got it so the priest left. A few minutes later, another woman entered and said, "Father forgive me for I have sinned."

The rabbi asked, "What did you do?" The woman replied, "I committed adultery."

The rabbi asked, "How many times?" The woman answered, "Once."

The rabbi said, "Go do it two more times. We have a special this week, three for $5.00."

Donations

Father O'Malley answers the phone.

"Hello, is this Father O'Malley?"

"It is."

"This is the IRS. Can you help us?"

"I can."

"Do you know a Ted Houlihan?"

"I do."

"Is he a member of your congregation?"

"He is."

"Did he donate $10,000.00 to the church?"

"He will."

Getting Ready for a Trip

A minister waited in line to have his car filled with gas just before a long holiday weekend. The attendant worked quickly, but there were many cars ahead of him at the service station. Finally, the attendant motioned him toward a vacant pump.

"Sorry about the delay, Reverend," said the young man. "It seems as if everyone waits until the last minute to get ready for a long trip."

The minister chuckled, "I know what you mean. It's the same in my business."

CHAPTER SIX

OUT OF THE MOUTHS OF BABES

As the saying goes, "Kids say the darndest things." Here are some jokes sure to bring a chuckle:

Dad Wins

A father of five children won a toy in a Mother's Day raffle. He called his kids together to decide which one of them should get the toy.

"Okay kids, who is the most obedient?" he asked. "Who never talks back to mother? Who does everything she says?"

"Okay, Dad," all five kids mumbled together as they shuffled off. "You get to have it."

Who Are You?

After playing outside all day, a little boy all covered in dirt came inside and marched up to his mother. "Guess who I am?"

"I give up," the mother replied. "Who are you?"

"Wow! Mrs. Johnson was right!" the boy squealed. "She said I was so dirty my own mother wouldn't recognize me."

Wise Advice

If you have trouble getting your children's attention, just sit down and look comfortable.

Five Truths Children Have Learned:

1. No matter how hard you try, you can't baptize cats.
2. When your Mom is mad at your Dad, don't let her brush your hair.
3. You can't trust dogs to watch your food.
4. Don't sneeze when someone is cutting your hair.
5. Never hold a dust-buster and a cat at the same time.

Where's the Baby?

For weeks, a six-year-old lad kept telling his first-grade teacher about the baby brother or sister that was expected at his house.

One day, the mother allowed the boy to feel the movements of the unborn child.

The six-year-old was obviously impressed, but made no comment. Furthermore, he stopped telling his teacher about the impending event.

The teacher finally sat the boy on her lap and said, "Tommy, whatever has become of that baby brother or sister you were expecting at home?"

Tommy burst into tears and confessed, "I think Mommy ate it!"

Test Answers

These are actual test answers given by kids of varying ages from different schools:

Q: Name the four seasons.
A: Salt, pepper, mustard, and vinegar.

Q: How is dew formed?
A: The sun shines down on the leaves and makes them   perspire.

Q: How can you delay milk turning sour?
A: Keep it in the cow.
Q: What does varicose mean?
A: Nearby.

Q: What is a terminal illness?
A: When you are sick at the airport.

Q: What does the word "benign" mean?
A: Benign is what you will be after you be eight.

Logical Answer

At a farmer's house, his young son, about 12, opened the door.

"Is yer Pa home?" the caller asked.

"No sir, he sure ain't," the boy replied. "He's gone to town."

"Well," said the visitor. "Is yer Ma home?"

"No, she ain't here neither. She went to town with Pa."

"Well, then, how about yer brother, Joe, is he here?"

"No sir, he went with Pa and Ma."

The caller stood there for a few minutes, shifting from one foot to the other and mumbling to himself.

"Is there anything I kin do fer ya?" inquired the young boy politely. "I know where all the tools are, if you want to borry one; or maybe I could take a message fer Pa."

"Well," said the other uncomfortably, "I really wanted to talk to yer Pa. It's about your brother, Joe, getting my daughter, Pearly Mae, pregnant."

The boy considered for a moment.

"Yep, you would have to talk to Pa about that," he finally conceded. "I know that Pa charges $50 for the bull and $25 for the boar hog, but I really don't know how much he gets for Joe."

20,000 Leagues Under the Sea

Our five-year-old grandson, Mark, couldn't wait to tell his father about the movie we had watched on television, "20,000 Leagues Under the Sea." The scenes with the submarine and the giant octopus had kept him wide-eyed.

My son interrupted Mark and asked, "What caused the submarine to sink?"

With a look of incredulity, Mark replied, "Dad, it was the 20,000 leaks!"

How You Make Babies

A second grader came home from school and said to her mother, "Guess what? We learned how to make babies today."

The mother, more than a little surprised, tried to keep her cool. "That's interesting," she said. "How do you make babies?"

"It's simple," replied the girl. "You just change 'y' to 'i' and add 'es.'"

To Tell the Truth

Little Johnny watched his Daddy's car pass by the school playground and go into the woods. Curious, he followed the car and saw Daddy and Aunt Jane in a passionate embrace. Little Johnny found this so exciting that he could not contain himself as he ran home and started to tell his mother.

"Mommy, I was at the playground and I saw Daddy go into the woods with Aunt Jane. I went back to look and he was giving Aunt Jane a big kiss, then he helped her take off her shirt. Then Aunt Jane helped Daddy take his pants off, then Aunt Jane ...."

At this point Mommy cut him off and said, "Johnny, this is such an interesting story. Suppose you save the rest of it for supper time. I want to see the look on Daddy's face when you tell it tonight."

At the dinner table, Mommy asked little Johnny to tell his story. Johnny started his story about the car going into the woods, the undressing, Aunt Jane lying down on the back seat.

"Then Aunt Jane and Daddy started doing the same thing that Mommy and Uncle Bill used to do when Daddy was in the Army."

Sometimes you need to listen to the whole story before you interrupt!

All in the Mind's Eye

The sixth grade science teacher, Mrs. Parks, asked her class, "Which human body part increases to 10 times its size when stimulated?"

No one answered until little Mary stood up and said, "You should not be asking sixth graders a question like that! I'm going to tell my parents, and they will go and tell the principal, who will then fire you!"

Mrs. Parks ignored her and asked the question again, "Which body part increases to 10 times its size when stimulated?"

Little Mary's mouth fell open. Then she said to those around her, "Boy, is she going to get in big trouble!"

The teacher continued to ignore her and said to the class, "Anybody?"

Finally, Billy stood up, looked around nervously, and said, "The body part that increases 10 times its size when stimulated is the pupil of the eye."

Mrs. Parks said, "Very good, Billy," then turned to Mary and continued. "As for you, young lady, I have three things to say: One, you have a dirty mind. Two, you didn't read your homework. And three, one day you are going to be very, very disappointed."

Horse Lessons

Little Johnny attended a horse auction with his father. He watched as his father moved from horse to horse, running his hands up and down the horse's legs, rump, and chest.

After a few minutes, Johnny asked, "Dad, why are you doing that?"

His father replied, "Because I'm buying horses. I have to make sure that they are healthy and in good shape before I buy."

Johnny looked worried, "Then I think we'd better hurry home right away."

"Why?" said his father.

"Because the UPS man stopped by yesterday. I think he wants to buy Mom."

The Good Ol' Days

A mother was telling her little girl what her own childhood was like.

"We used to skate outside on a pond. I had a swing made from a tire; it hung from a tree in our front yard. We rode our pony. We picked wild raspberries in the woods."

The little girl was wide-eyed, taking this in.

At last she said, "I sure wish I'd gotten to know you sooner!"

What is Love?

A group of professional people posed this question to a group of four- to eight-year-olds, "What does love mean?" The answers they got were broader and deeper than anyone could have imagined. See what you think:

1. When my grandmother got arthritis, she couldn't bend over and paint her toenails anymore. So my grandfather does it for her all the time, even when his hands got arthritis too. That's love.
    Rebecca – Age 8

2. When someone loves you, the way they say your name is different. You know that your name is safe in their mouth.
    Billy – Age 4

3. Love is when a girl puts on perfume and a boy puts on shaving cologne and they go out and smell each other.
Karl – Age 5

4. Love is when you go out to eat and give somebody most of your French fries without making them give you any of theirs.
Chrissy – Age 6

5. Love is what makes you smile when you're tired. Terri – Age 4

6. Love is when my mommy makes coffee for my daddy and she takes a sip before giving it to him, to make sure the taste is okay.
Danny – Age 7

7. Love is when you kiss all the time. Then when you get tired of kissing, you still want to be together and you talk more. My Mommy and Daddy are like that. They look gross when they kiss.
Emily – Age 8

8. Love is what's in the room with you at Christmas if you stop opening presents and listen.
Bobby – Age 7

9. If you want to learn to love better, you should start with a friend who you hate.
Nikka – Age 6

10. There are two kinds of love. Our love. God's love. But God makes both kinds of them.
Jenny – Age 8

11. Love is when you tell a guy you like his shirt, and then he wears it every day.
Noelle – Age 7

12. Love is like a little old woman and a little old man who are still friends even after they know each other so well.
Tommy – Age 6

13. During my piano recital, I was on a stage and I was scared. I looked at all the people watching me and saw my daddy waving and smiling. He was the only one doing that. I wasn't scared anymore.
Cindy – Age 8

14. My mommy loves me more than anybody. You don't see anyone else kissing me to sleep at night. Clare – Age 6

15. Love is when Mommy gives Daddy the best piece of chicken.
Elaine – Age 5

16. Love is when Mommy sees Daddy smelly and sweaty and still says he is handsomer than Robert Redford.
Chris – Age 7

17. Love is when your puppy licks your face even after you left him alone all day.
Mary Ann – Age 4

18. I know my older sister loves me because she gives me all her old clothes and has to go out and buy new ones.
Lauren – Age 4

19. When you love somebody, your eyelashes go up and down and little stars come out of you.
Karen – Age 7

20. Love is when Mommy sees Daddy on the toilet and she doesn't think it's gross.
Mark – Age 6

21. You really shouldn't say 'I love you' unless you mean it. But if you mean it, you should say it a lot. People forget.
Jennifer – Age 8

The Most Caring Child

Author and lecturer Leo Buscaglia once talked about a contest he was asked to judge. The purpose of the contest was to find the most caring child.

The winner was a four-year-old child whose next door neighbor was an elderly gentleman who had recently lost his wife. Upon seeing the man cry, the little boy went into the old gentleman's yard, climbed onto his lap, and just sat there.

When his Mother asked him what he had said to the neighbor, the little boy said, "Nothing, I just helped him cry."

Jewish Mothers

- MONA LISA'S JEWISH MOTHER:
  "This you call a smile, after all the money your father and I spent on braces?"

- CHRISTOPHER COLUMBUS'S JEWISH MOTHER:

"I don't care what you've discovered, you still should have written!"

- MICHELANGELO'S JEWISH MOTHER:
  "Why can't you paint on walls like other children? Do you know how hard it is to get this junk off the ceiling?"

- NAPOLEON'S JEWISH MOTHER:
  "All right, if you're not hiding your report card inside your jacket, take your hand out of there and show me!"

- ABRAHAM LINCOLN'S JEWISH MOTHER:
  "Again with the hat! Why can't you wear a baseball cap like the other kids?"

- GEORGE WASHINGTON'S JUEWISH MOTHER:
  "Next time I catch you throwing money across the Potomac, you can kiss your allowance goodbye!"

- THOMAS EDISON'S JEWISH MOTHER:
  "Of course I'm proud that you invented the electric light bulb. Now, turn it off and go to sleep!"

Pssst...

A kindergarten pupil told his teacher he'd found a cat. She asked him if it was dead or alive.

"Dead," she was informed.

"How do you know?" she asked her pupil.

"Because I pissed in its ear and it didn't move," answered the child innocently.

"You did WHAT?" the teacher exclaimed in surprise.

"You know," explained the boy. "I leaned over and went 'Pssst' and it didn't move."

CHAPTER
SEVEN

DOG GONE IT!

Let's face it; animals were created to make us smile. If you have a pet, you must have a sense of humor. With that in mind, I share the following pet humor with you:

Thinking Fast

Two men are walking their dogs, a poodle and a German Shepard. They decide they'd like to go into a bar for a drink.

"But we can't bring dogs into that bar," says the poodle's human.

"Hey, no problem," says the German Shepard's owner. "Just watch this." He pulls out a pair of sunglasses and walks into the bar.

"Hey, no dogs!" yells the bartender.

"But this is a seeing eye dog," says the German Shepard's human. The bartender apologizes and shows them to a chair.

So, the poodle owner decides to follow suit, whips out his sunglasses, and walks into the bar.

"Hey, no dogs!" yells the bartender.

"But this is a seeing eye dog," says the poodle's human.

The bartender objects, "Hey, poodles can't be seeing eye dogs!"

The poodle owner gasps, "Poodle? They told me they were giving me a German Shepard!"

Dogs and Fleas

Q: What's expected if a dog goes to a flea circus?

A: He will steal the show!

A Hunting Dog

A Mustang (Officer-former enlisted), retired after 35 years, realized a lifelong dream of buying a bird-hunting estate in

Alaska. He invited an old Admiral friend to visit for a week of pheasant shooting.

The friend was in awe of the Mustang's new gun dog, "Chief." The dog could point, flush, and retrieve with the very best. The Admiral offered to buy the dog at any price.

The Mustang declined, saying that Chief was the very best bird dog he had ever owned and that he couldn't part with him.

Six months later, the same Admiral returned for another week of hunting and was surprised to find the Mustang breaking in a new dog. "What happened to Chief?" he asked.

"Had to shoot him," the Mustang replied. "Another old shipmate came to hunt with me and couldn't remember the dog's name. He kept calling him 'Master Chief.' After that, all the dog would do was sit on his butt and bark."

Obedience School

During break time at obedience school, two dogs were talking.

One said to the other: "The thing I hate about obedience school is you learn ALL this stuff you will never use in the real world."

Hair Removal

My neighbor found out her dog could hardly hear so she took it to the veterinarian. He found the problem was hair in its ears and cleaned both ears and the dog could hear fine.

The vet told the lady if she wanted to keep this from reoccurring she should go to the store and get some 'Nair' hair remover and rub it in its ears once a month.

The lady goes to the drug store and gets some 'Nair' hair remover. At the register, the druggist tells her, "If you're going to use this under your arms don't use deodorant for a few days."

The lady says, "I'm not using it under my arms."

The druggist says, "If you're using it on your legs, don't shave for a couple of days."

The lady says, "I'm not using it on my legs either. If you must know, I'm using it on my schnauzer."

The druggist says, "Stay off your bicycle for a week."

The Difference between Dogs and Cats

Dogs have owners.

Cats have staff.

Dumb Blondes

Returning from work, a blonde was shocked to find her house ransacked and burglarized. She telephoned the police at once and reported the crime.

The police dispatcher broadcast the crime on the channels and a K-9 unit patrolling nearby was the first to respond.

As the K-9 office approached the house with his dog on a leash, the blonde ran out on the porch, shuddered at the sight of the cop and his dog, then sat down on the steps.

Putting her face in her hands, she moaned, "I come home to find all my possessions stolen. I call the police for help and what do they do? They send me a BLIND policeman."

Talking Dog for Sale

A guy sees a sign in front of a house: "Talking Dog for Sale."

He rings the bell and the owner tells him the dog is in the backyard. The guy goes into the backyard and sees a black mutt just sitting there.

"You talk?" he asks.

"Sure do!" the dog replies.

"So, what's your story?"

The dog looks up and says, "Well, I discovered my gift of talking pretty young and I wanted to help the government, so I told the CIA about my gift, and in no time they had me jetting from country to country, sitting in rooms with spies and world leaders, because no one figured a dog would be eavesdropping. I was one of their most valuable spies eight years running. The jetting around really tired me out, and I know I wasn't getting any younger and I wanted to settle down. So I signed up for a job at the airport to do some undercover security work, mostly wandering near suspicious characters and listening in. I uncovered some incredible dealings there and was awarded a batch of medals. Had a wife, a mess of puppies, and now I'm just retired."

The guy is amazed. He goes back in and asks the owner what he wants for the dog.

The owner says, "Ten dollars."

The guy says, "This dog is amazing. Why on earth are you selling him so cheap?"

"Cause he's a liar. He didn't do any of that stuff."

Have You Ever Wondered...

Did you ever notice that when you blow in a dog's face, he gets mad at you, but when you take him on a car ride, he sticks his head out the window?

Winner of the Best Singles Ad

The following was in The Atlanta Journal. This has got to be one of the best "singles ads" ever:

SINGLE BLACK FEMALE seeks male companionship, ethnicity unimportant. I'm a very good looking girl who LOVES to play. I love long walks in the woods, riding in your pickup truck, hunting, camping and fishing trips, and cozy winter nights lying by the fire. Candlelight dinners will have me eating out of your hand. Rub me the right way and watch me respond. I'll be at the front door when you get home from work wearing only what nature gave me. Kiss me and I'm yours. Call (404) 875-6420 and ask for Daisy.

Over 15,000 men found themselves talking to the Atlanta Humane Society about an eight-week old black Labrador retriever.

Why Dogs Are Better Than Men

1. Dogs don't have problems expressing affection in public.

2. Dogs miss you when you're gone.

3. Dogs feel guilty when they've done something wrong.

4. Dogs admit when they're jealous.

5. Dogs are very direct about wanting to go out.

6. Dogs don't play games with you – except fetch – and they never laugh at how you throw.

7. You can train a dog.

8. Dogs are easy to buy for.

9. The worst social disease you can get from dogs is fleas.

10. Dogs understand what "no" means.

11. Dogs mean it when they kiss you.

How Men and Dogs Are Equal:

1. Neither of them notice when you get your hair cut.

2. Both want to be dominant.

3. Both are suspicious of the postman.

Heavenly Dogs

A man and his dog were walking along a road. The man was enjoying the scenery, when it suddenly occurred to him that he was dead.

He remembered dying, and that the dog walking beside him had been dead for years. He wondered where the road was leading them.

After a while, they came to a high, white stone wall along one side of the road. It looked like fine marble. At the top of a long hill, it was broken by a tall arch that glowed in the sunlight.

When he was standing before it, he saw a magnificent gate in the arch that looked like mother-of-pearl, and the street that led to the gate looked like pure gold. He and the dog walked toward the gate, and as he got closer, he saw a man at a desk behind the gate.

When he was close enough, he called out, "Excuse me, where are we?"

"This is Heaven, sir," the man answered.

"Wow! Would you happen to have some water?" the man asked.

"Of course, sir. Come right in, and I'll have some ice water brought right up."

The man gestured, and the gate began to open.

"Can my friend," gesturing toward his dog, "come in, too?" the traveler asked.

"I'm sorry, sir, but we don't allow pets."

The man thought a moment and then turned back toward the road and continued the way he had been going with his dog.

After another long walk, and at the top of another long hill, he came to a dirt road leading through a farm gate that looked as if it had never been closed. There was no fence. As he approached the gate, he saw a man inside, leaning against a tree and reading a book.

"Excuse me!" he called to the man. "Do you have any water?"

"Yeah, sure, there's a pump over there, come on in."

"How about my friend here?" the traveler gestured to the dog.

"There should be a bowl by the pump."

They went through the gate, and sure enough, there was an old-fashioned hand pump with a bowl beside it. The traveler filled the water bowl and took a long drink himself, then he gave some to the dog. When they were full, he and the dog walked back toward the man who was standing by the tree.

"What do you call this place?" the traveler asked.

"This is Heaven," he answered.

"Well, that's confusing," the traveler said. "The man down the road said that was Heaven, too."

"Oh, you mean the place with the gold street and pearly gates? Nope. That's hell."

"Doesn't it make you mad for them to use your name like that?"

"No, we're just happy that they screen out the folks who would leave their best friends behind."

CHAPTER EIGHT

WHY IS IT SO?

Some things make absolutely no sense. Which leads us to the inevitable question:

Why, oh, Why?

Why do we press harder on a remote control when we know the batteries are going dead?

Why do they use sterilized needles for death by lethal injection?

Whose idea was it to put an "S" in the word "lisp"?

Is there ever a day when mattresses are NOT on sale?

Why do Kamikaze pilots wear helmets?

Who was the first person to look at a cow and say, "I think I'll squeeze these pink dangly things here and drink whatever comes out?"

Why do people constantly return to the refrigerator with the hopes that something new to eat will have materialized?

How come when you first pull the drapery cord, the drapes always move the wrong way?

Why do people keep running over a string a dozen times with their vacuum cleaner, reach down, pick it up, examine it, and then put it down to give their vacuum one more chance?

How do those dead bugs get into closed light fixtures?

Why do women always ask questions that have no right answers?

Why do old men wear their pants higher than younger men?

Why is it that inside every older person is a younger person wondering what the heck happened?

If Barbie is so popular, why do you have to buy her friends?

Who was the first person to say, "See that chicken there? I'm going to eat the next thing that comes out of its bum."

Why does your Obstetrician or Gynecologist leave the room when you get undressed if they are going to look up there anyway?

Why are the needy only thought of during the holidays? Aren't they just as needy the rest of the year?

Why do men refer to a broken bone as 'just a sprain' and a deep wound as 'just a scratch,' but when they get the sniffles they are deathly ill 'with the flu' and have to be bed-ridden for weeks?

Why don't we ever hear any father-in-law jokes?

Why do men forget everything and women remember everything?

Words of Wisdom

Don't worry about what people think; they don't do it very often.

Going to a church doesn't make you a Christian any more than standing in a garage makes you a car.

It isn't the jeans that make your butt look fat.

Not one shred of evidence supports the notion that life is serious.

It is easier to get forgiveness than permission.

For every action, there is an equal and opposite government program.

If you look like your passport picture, you probably need the trip.

Bills travel through the mail at twice the speed of checks.

A conscience is what hurts when all your other parts feel good.

Eat well, stay fit, and die anyway. (Just remember how lucky you were to get a free trip around the sun.)

Men are from earth. Women are from earth. Deal with it.

No man has ever been shot while doing the dishes.

A balanced diet is a cookie in each hand.

Middle age is when broadness of the mind and narrowness of the waist change places.

Junk is something you've kept for years and throw away about three weeks before you need it.

There is always one more imbecile than you counted on.

Watch Where You Step

The owner of the carriage obviously had a sense of humor, because attached to the back of the carriage was a hand printed sign:

"Energy efficient vehicle: Runs on oats and grass. Caution: Do not step in exhaust."

Roe vs. Wade

A young man was sitting in class when the professor asked him if he knew what the Roe vs. Wade decision was. He sat quietly, pondering this profound question.

Finally, after giving it a lot of thought, he sighed and said, "I think this was the decision George Washington made prior to crossing the Delaware."

Truisms

My husband and I divorced over religious differences. He thought he was God and I didn't.

I don't suffer from insanity; I enjoy every minute of it.

I work hard because millions on welfare depend on me.

Some people are alive only because it's illegal to kill them.

I used to have a handle on life, but it broke.

I'm not a complete idiot—some parts are missing.

God must love stupid people; he made so many.

It is as BAD as you think and they ARE out to get you.

Consciousness: that annoying time between naps.

Ever stop to think, and forget to start again?

Wrinkled was not one of the things I wanted to be when I grew up.

Procrastinate now!

My dog can lick anyone.

West Virginia: one million people and 15 last names.

A hangover is the wrath of grapes.

He who dies with the most toys is nonetheless dead.

Time's fun when you're having flies, said Kermit the Frog.

Police station toilet stolen. Cops have nothing to go on.

Why We Hate HMO

Here are 10 sure signs that your employer has switched to a cheaper HMO:

1. Your annual breast exam is done at Hooters.

2. Directions to your Doctor's office include, "Take a left when you enter the trailer park."

3. The tongue depressors taste faintly of Fudgesicles.

4. The only proctologist in the plan is "Gus" from Roto-Rooter.

5. The only item listed under Preventative Care coverage is: "An apple a day."

6. Your primary care physician is wearing the pants you gave to Goodwill last month.

7. "The patient is responsible for 200% of out of network charges," is not a typographical error.

8. The only expense covered 100% is embalming.

9. Your Prozac comes in different colors with little M's on them.

10. You ask for Viagra, and they give you a Popsicle stick and duct tape.

Funny [Actual] Headlines

Crack Found on Governor's Daughter

Something Went Wrong in Jet Crash, Expert Says

Police Begin Campaign to Run Down Jaywalkers

Iraqi Head Seeks Arms

Is There a Ring of Debris around Uranus?

Prostitutes Appeal to Pope

Panda Mating Fails; Veterinarian Takes Over

Teacher Strikes Idle Kids
Miners Refuse to Work after Death

Juvenile Court to Try Shooting Defendant

War Dims Hope for Peace

If Strike Isn't Settled Quickly, It May Last Awhile

Cold Wave Linked to Temperatures

Enfield (London) Couple Slain; Police Suspect Homicide

Red Tape Holds Up New Bridges

Man Stuck By Lightning Faces Battery Charge

New Study of Obesity Looks for Larger Test Group

Astronaut Takes Blame for Gas in Spacecraft

Kids Make Nutritious Snacks

Chef Throws His Heart into Helping Feed Needy

Local High School Dropouts Cut in Half

Hospitals are Sued by Seven Foot Doctors

Typhoon Rips through Cemetery; Hundreds Dead

More Funny Stuff

Ham and eggs – A day's work for a chicken, a lifetime commitment for a pig.

Never take life seriously. Nobody gets out alive anyway.

Life is sexually transmitted.

Give a person a fish and you feed them for a day; teach a person to use the internet and they won't bother you for weeks.

Whenever I feel blue, I start breathing again.

Why does a slight tax increase cost you two hundred dollars and a substantial tax cut saves you thirty cents?

In the 60's, people took acid to make the world weird. Now the weird people take Prozac to make it normal.

Play on Words

Those who jump off a bridge in Paris are in Seine.

A backward poet writes inverse.

A man's home is his castle in a manor of speaking.

Dijon vu – the same mustard as before.

Practice safe eating – always use condiments.

Shotgun wedding: A case of wife or death.

A man needs a mistress just to break the monogamy.

Dancing cheek-to-cheek is really a form of floor play.

Does the name Pavlov ring a bell?

Condoms should be used on every conceivable occasion.

Reading while sunbathing makes you well red.

When two egotists meet, it's an 'I' for an 'I.'

A bicycle can't stand on its own because it is two tired.

The definition of a will? It's a giveaway.

Time flies like an arrow. Fruit flies like a banana.

In democracy your vote counts. In feudalism your Count votes.

A chicken crossing the road is poultry in motion.

If you don't pay your exorcist, you get repossessed.

With her marriage, she got a new name and a dress.

When a clock is hungry, it goes back four seconds.

The man who fell into an upholstery machine is fully recovered.

You feel stuck with your debt if you can't budge it.

Local Area Network in Australia: The LAN down under.

He often broke into song because he couldn't find the key.

Every calendar's days are numbered.

A lot of money is tainted. It taint yours and it taint mine.

A boiled egg in the morning is hard to beat.

He had a photographic memory that was never developed.

A plateau is a high form of flattery.

A midget fortune teller who escapes from prison is a small medium at large.

Those who get too big for their britches will be exposed in the end.

Once you've seen one shopping center, you've seen a mall.

Bakers trade bread recipes on a knead-to-know basis.

Santa's helpers are subordinate clauses.

Acupuncture is a jab well done.

Exact Duplicates

I'd kill for a Nobel Peace Prize.

Borrow money from pessimists; they don't expect it back.

Half the people you know are below average.

Ninety-nine percent of lawyers give the rest a bad name.

About 42.7% of all statistics are made up on the spot.
A conscience is what hurts when all your other parts feel so good.

A clear conscience is usually the sign of a bad memory.

If you want the rainbow, you have to put up with the rain.

All those who believe in psycho-kinesis, raise my hand.

The early bird may get the worm, but the second mouse gets the cheese.

I almost had a psychic girlfriend but she left me before we met.

Okay, so what's the speed of dark?

How do you tell when you're out of invisible ink?

If everything seems to be going well, you have obviously overlooked something.

Depression is merely anger without enthusiasm.

When everything is coming your way, you're in the wrong lane.

Ambition is a poor excuse for not having enough sense to be lazy.

Hard work pays off in the future, but laziness pays off now.

I intend to live forever – so far, so good.

Eagles may soar, but weasels don't get sucked into jet engines.

What happens if you get scared half to death twice?

My mechanic told me, "I couldn't repair your brakes, so I made your horn louder."

Why do psychics have to ask for your name?

If at first you don't succeed, destroy all evidence that you tried.

A conclusion is the place where you got tired of thinking.

Experience is something you don't get until just after you need it.

The hardness of the butter is proportional to the softness of the bread.

To steal ideas from one person is plagiarism; to steal from many is research.

The problem with the gene pool is that there is no lifeguard.

The sooner you fall behind, the more time you'll have to catch up.

Silly Signs

- Spotted in a toilet of a London office:
  Toilet out of order. Please use floor below.

- In a Laundromat:
  Automatic washing machines: Please remove all your clothes when the light goes out.

- In a London department store:
  Bargain basement upstairs.

- In an office:
  Would the person who took the step ladder yesterday please bring it back or further steps will be taken.

- In an office:
  After tea break, staff should empty the teapot and stand upside down on the draining board.

- Outside a secondhand shop:
  We exchange anything – bicycles, washing machines, etc. Why not bring your wife along and get a wonderful bargain?

- Notice in health food shop window:

Closed due to illness.

- Spotted in a safari park:
  Elephants please stay in your car.

- Seen during a conference:
  For anyone who has children and doesn't know it, there is a day care on the 1st floor.

- Notice in a farmer's field:
  The farmer allows walkers to cross the field for free, but the bull charges.

- Message on a leaflet:
  If you cannot read, this leaflet will tell you how to get lessons.

- On a repair shop door:
  We can repair anything. (Please knock hard on the door- the bell doesn't work.)

That's All Folks!

Alas, all good things must come to an end. As the famous last line of the Loony-Tune cartoons says, "That's all folks!"

That is, until Volume II comes out!

Until then, I hope you enjoyed these jokes as much as I enjoyed sharing them with you.